The illustrations for this book were made with acrylic paint on paper.

Cataloging-in-Publication Data has been applied for and
may be obtained from the Library of Congress.

ISBN 978-1-4197-5681-8

Text and illustrations © 2023 Marc Majewski
Book design by Pamela Notarantonio

Published in 2023 by Abrams Books for Young Readers, an imprint
of ABRAMS. All rights reserved. No portion of this book may
be reproduced, stored in a retrieval system, or transmitted in any form
or by any means, mechanical, electronic, photocopying, recording,
or otherwise, without written permission from the publisher.

Printed and bound in China
10 9 8 7 6 5 4 3 2 1

Abrams Books for Young Readers are available at special discounts when
purchased in quantity for premiums and promotions as well as
fundraising or educational use. Special editions can also be created to
specification. For details, contact specialsales@abramsbooks.com
or the address below.

Abrams® is a registered trademark of Harry N. Abrams, Inc.

ABRAMS The Art of Books
195 Broadway, New York, NY 10007
abramsbooks.com

BRIDGES

Marc Majewski

Abrams Books for Young Readers

New York

BRIDGES ARE HIGH
Millau Viaduct, FRANCE

This bridge is even taller than the Eiffel Tower!

BRIDGES ARE LOW
Bow Bridge, USA

This bridge is one of the most romantic spots for New Yorkers.

BRIDGES ARE LONG
Hong Kong-Zhuhai-Macau Bridge, China

This bridge is the longest sea-crossing bridge in the world!

BRiDGES ARE SHORT
El Marco Bridge, Spain - Portugal

On this bridge, it only takes a few
steps to cross from Spain to Portugal.

BRiDGES ARE STRAiGHT
Lake Pontchartrain Causeway, USA

This bridge cuts the lake right through the middle.

BRIDGES ARE CURVY
Python Bridge, Netherlands

On summer days, this bridge is a good spot for diving.

BRIDGES STAND OUT
Golden Gate Bridge, USA

The unmistakable color of this bridge is called "international orange."

BRIDGES BLEND IN
Umshiang Double-Decker Root Bridge, India

This living bridge grows and gets stronger year after year.

BRIDGES ARE SUSPENDED
Charles Kuonen Suspension Bridge, Switzerland

This is the longest suspension bridge in the Alps.

BRIDGES ARE SUBMERGED
Moses Bridge, Netherlands

Look closely—this bridge is almost invisible!

BRiDGES STAND FiRM
Akashi Kaikyo Bridge, Japan

The wind may huff and puff—but it will never blow this bridge down!

BRIDGES SWING
Carrick-a-Rede Rope Bridge, Northern Ireland

I wouldn't look down from this bridge if I were you!

BRIDGES OPEN UP
Tower Bridge, United Kingdom

This bridge opens around 800 times a year!

BRIDGES ROTATE
Woman's Bridge, Argentina

This bridge's design was inspired by a couple dancing the tango.

BRIDGES LINK COUNTRIES

Victoria Falls Bridge, Zambia - Zimbabwe

On one side, Zambia; on the other, Zimbabwe.

BRIDGES LINK CONTINENTS
Bosphorus Bridge, Turkey

On one side, Europe; on the other, Asia.

BRIDGES TELL STORIES
Ponte della Maddalena
Or "Devil's Bridge," Italy

It is said that the Devil himself helped build this bridge . . .

BRiDGES MARK HiSTORY
Edmund Pettus Bridge, USA

This bridge has become an important landmark
of the civil rights movement.

EDMUND PE

This bridge is almost 2,000 years old.

BRIDGES INSPIRE
Giverny Japanese Footbridge, France

This bridge inspired the painter Claude Monet
to create some of his most famous paintings.

Brooklyn Bridge, USA

ALL OVER THE WORLD,
BRIDGES CONNECT...

ABOUT THE BRIDGES

BRIDGES ARE HIGH
Millau Viaduct, FRANCE

The Millau Viaduct is a cable-stayed bridge, a type of bridge where the deck is suspended by cables which are supported by one or more towers. It rises above the little town of Millau, France. With a height of 1,125 feet, it is the tallest bridge in the world!

BRIDGES ARE LOW
Bow Bridge, USA

The Bow Bridge is a pedestrian bridge that gracefully crosses the Lake in Central Park, New York City, USA. The bridge is distinguished by its elegant and low arch shape, which resembles a violinist's bow. It is also a popular spot for wedding proposals!

BRIDGES ARE LONG
Hong Kong–Zhuhai–Macau Bridge, China

The Hong Kong–Zhuhai–Macau Bridge is made up of a group of bridges and tunnels connecting the cities of Hong Kong, Zhuhai, and Macau. It is divided into three sections: the Main Bridge (18.4 miles), the Hong Kong Link Road (7.5 miles), and the Zhuhai Link Road (8.3 miles), adding up to a total length of 34 miles. That makes it the longest sea-crossing bridge in the world!

BRIDGES ARE SHORT
El Marco Bridge, Spain–Portugal

El Marco Bridge is a small pedestrian bridge that connects the municipalities of La Codosera in Spain and Arronches in Portugal. With a length of only 10.5 feet, El Marco Bridge is the shortest international bridge in the world. For many years, the bridge was made of wooden planks that would sink into the river on rainy days! Finally, in 2008, the bridge was modernized and made safer for people to cross.

BRIDGES ARE STRAIGHT
Lake Pontchartrain Causeway, USA

The Lake Pontchartrain Causeway in Louisiana is composed of twin parallel bridges 23.8 miles long, with traffic on each going in the opposite direction of the other. Before the construction of the bridge, driving around the big Lake Pontchartrain was very time-consuming. It became obvious that the shortest way to reach the other side of the lake was to cut right through the middle. The bridge is so long that drivers on one end of it can't even see the other side!

BRIDGES ARE CURVY
Python Bridge, Netherlands

The Python Bridge, officially known as the High Bridge, is a pedestrian bridge that crosses the canal between the neighborhoods of Sporenburg and Borneo Isle in Amsterdam. Its nickname comes from its unusual, wavy shape that looks like a big snake!

BRIDGES STAND OUT
Golden Gate Bridge, USA

The Golden Gate Bridge is a suspension bridge, a type of bridge where the deck is suspended by cables passing over two tall towers and anchored at both ends. It majestically crosses the Golden Gate, a strait linking the Pacific Ocean to the San Francisco Bay. The bridge is famous for its vivid color, called "international orange," which was selected to enhance the bridge's visibility.

BRIDGES BLEND IN
Umshiang Double-Decker Root Bridge, India

Living root bridges are handmade bridges grown from living plant roots. They are very common in Meghalaya, a state in northeastern India. There, they are built by the Khasi and Jaintia communities through a process called "tree-shaping." This technique consists of knotting and guiding the aerial roots of rubber trees into the shape of a bridge, whose structure continues to grow and strengthen year after year. It takes between 15 and 45 years to create a living root bridge. And even without the use of a single nail, they can last more than 500 years!

BRIDGES ARE SUSPENDED
Charles Kuonen Suspension Bridge, Switzerland

The Charles Kuonen Suspension Bridge is a simple suspension bridge: Unlike other suspension bridges, it has no tower, and its deck is solely suspended by the cables anchored at both ends. Over 1,600 feet long and up to 280 feet high, it is part of a long hiking trail between Grächen and Zermatt in Switzerland, and it is only accessible to hikers!

BRIDGES ARE SUBMERGED
Moses Bridge, Netherlands

Crossing the moat of the Fort de Roovere in Halsteren, Netherlands, the unusual, fascinating Moses Bridge is almost invisible because it is totally below the waterline! When it was originally built, the moat surrounding the fortress provided a first line of defense against enemies. It was either dry or flooded with water, and it had no bridge to cross it. As part of a renovation project, a sunken bridge was built with waterproof wood to give access to the fortress while preserving the site's original aesthetic. The bridge was named for the way it parts the water like the biblical figure Moses.

BRIDGES STAND FIRM
Akashi Kaikyo Bridge, Japan

The Akashi Kaikyo Bridge, also called Pearl Bridge, is a suspension bridge that connects the cities of Kobe and Iwaya, Japan. Despite its delicate nickname, this bridge is one of the longest, tallest, and strongest bridges in the world! It was designed to withstand violent earthquakes up to 8.5 on the Richter scale, and storms with winds of 178 miles per hour that constantly threaten the region of the Akashi strait.

BRIDGES SWING
Carrick-a-Rede Rope Bridge, Northern Ireland

The Carrick-a-Rede Rope Bridge is a rope bridge that connects the mainland of Northern Ireland's cliffs to the island of Carrick-a-Rede. It spans 66 feet and sways 98 feet above the sea. The bridge was first built by salmon fishermen about 350 years ago. Today, it is mostly used by tourists, who cross this swinging little bridge made solely of rope and wooden planks.

BRIDGES OPEN UP
Tower Bridge, United Kingdom

Tower Bridge is a combined suspension and bascule bridge. A bascule bridge is a type of movable bridge that can split in two and raise its sides up to allow boat traffic to pass through. Spanning the River Thames, Tower Bridge is one of the most iconic landmarks in London.

BRIDGES ROTATE
Woman's Bridge, Argentina

Puente de la Mujer, or "Woman's Bridge," is a rotating pedestrian bridge, also called a swing bridge: a type of movable bridge that can rotate horizontally. It was named in honor of the prominent Argentine women who also give their names to most streets in this district of Buenos Aires. The central section of the bridge can rotate ninety degrees to allow for the passage of boats.

BRIDGES LINK COUNTRIES
Victoria Falls Bridge, Zambia - Zimbabwe

The Victoria Falls Bridge is an arch bridge that sits 420 feet above the gorge of the waterfall, and it carries pedestrian, rail, and automobile traffic between Zambia and Zimbabwe. It is the only rail link between the two countries. Today, it is one of the most popular landmarks in the region, and tourists come every year to enjoy the breathtaking view of the Zambezi River and catch a spray from the waterfall.

BRIDGES LINK CONTINENTS
Bosphorus Bridge, Turkey

The Bosphorus Bridge, also called the 15 July Martyrs Bridge, is a suspension bridge that crosses the Bosphorus Strait, which also marks the boundary between Europe and Asia within Turkey. The idea of creating a link across the Bosphorus isn't new; a first attempt was made in 511 BCE by the Persian ruler Darius the Great, and another by Leonardo da Vinci, who designed a suspension bridge in about 1503 that was never built. It was only in 1973 that the Bosphorus Bridge became the first bridge to connect the two continents.

BRIDGES TELL STORIES
Ponte della Maddalena Or "Devil's Bridge," Italy

Ponte della Maddalena, also called "Devil's Bridge," is a pedestrian bridge crossing the Serchio River in Italy. "Devil's Bridge" refers to many bridges built across Europe during medieval times. Because of their extraordinary architecture, it was said that the Devil himself had helped in their construction. Each of these bridges has its own folktale associated with it. The legends are often similar, and frequently start with a pact made with the Devil to build the bridge in exchange for the soul of the first creature who would cross it. Once the bridge was completed, the builder would trick the Devil by making an animal walk across it first, and not a human as expected.

BRIDGES MARK HISTORY
Edmund Pettus Bridge, USA

The Edmund Pettus Bridge is an arch bridge that crosses the Alabama River in Selma, Alabama. The bridge was the site of Bloody Sunday on March 7, 1965, when civil rights marchers led by activists Hosea Williams and John Lewis were brutally attacked by police. It was named after Edmund Pettus, a former Confederate general, US senator, and a leader of the Ku Klux Klan. There have since been calls to rename the bridge for Lewis instead. Many marches have commemorated the events of Bloody Sunday; the bridge has become a National Historic Landmark and a symbol of the civil rights movement and the Black American struggle for equality.

BRIDGES REMEMBER
Pont du Gard, France

The Pont du Gard is an ancient Roman aqueduct bridge, which is a structure that conducts water across land to supply cities. It was built during the first century CE to transport water to the ancient Roman city of Nemausus (today called Nîmes). Though it no longer carries water, it is the best-preserved example of bridges built during ancient times, and is also the highest Roman aqueduct in the world, rising up to 160 feet!

BRIDGES INSPIRE
Giverny Japanese Footbridge, France

This wooden bridge is located in the water garden that belonged to the French impressionist painter Claude Monet, in Giverny—northwest of Paris, France—where he lived with his family. Monet's lush garden and its Japanese-style footbridge inspired him to create hundreds of paintings, including his famous series *Japanese Footbridge* and *Water Lilies*.

BRIDGES CONNECT
Brooklyn Bridge, USA

The Brooklyn Bridge is a hybrid suspension/cable-stayed bridge that spans the East River and connects Brooklyn and Manhattan in New York City. At the time of its construction, Brooklyn and Manhattan were two different cities, and the bridge was built to facilitate traffic between them. It was only in 1898 that Brooklyn became part of New York City. Every day, thousands of vehicles, bikers, and pedestrians cross the bridge to go from one borough to the other. Over the years, the bridge has become an iconic landmark of the city and one of the most famous bridges in the world.

Other Bridges Shown

COVER UNDER THE JACKET:
Manhattan Bridge, USA

TITLE PAGE:
El Marco Bridge, Spain - Portugal